MariGold

DAEIZM (DAE D. LEE)

DEDICATION

To my family,
my love, everyone that has supported me,
loved me, left me, returned, appeared briefly.
You've all taught me something I'll never forget.
You all were some kind of motivation to bring me to this point.
& Lil' Saint.

CONTENTS

ACKNOWLEDGMENTS

I want to take this time to thank **you**.
Yes, you, reading this.
These words are for you, too.
So that you may find strength
on the days you dread getting out of bed.
For beauty when you feel
too ashamed to look in the mirror.
So that you feel love even
when it no longer feels in your favor.

To remind you that you can.
That you are.

The book features selected short proverbs, prose
and poems that deal with love in multiple forms
from the grieving process of inner conflict and self love,
the hurdles of lust, heartbreak, new love,
love for our skin and circumstance,
and love through understanding those
broken pieces we all share and come from.
Grief-
ultimately breeds the growth within us;
whether it be through the aforementioned
or through something else, grieving helps us understand
where our pain comes from and can rain down enlightenment,
self-worth, liberation, and reflections.

I:
PLIGHT

marigold (intro)

Wrap me in your embers,
hold me from the light, marigold.
You tell me why search for
what will have me engulfed in
you in such a manner of time?
Why chase what will exhaust
you in our eventualities?
You tell me you are
what's best for me.
My reality.
My likely.
My devil with enticing remedies
with contingencies finely
tattooed beneath your bosom.
You tell me you are here to save me
yet shackle me from the
gold-laced horizon i desperately crave.
I know they're all lies—
yet i can never resist your lullabies.
Tell me once more how I'm destined to
be rooted in your caramel fires.

carry

"You carry too much", She said.
"The weight of the world was
not meant to be taken on.
How can you expect to enjoy life
when you're so caught up in
saving it from itself?"

marigold: father

I didn't tell the story of my father passing
because I felt that it wasn't news.
Where I'm from, they say that you're lucky to have one that wants you,
or one that isn't taken from you in an archaic war where our skin and
residence are enemy #1. Where the adage was:
"You never make it to 25",
and he was 23 and the odds weren't much for underdogs so his fate was
like grasping at straws, knowing they all were the small ones.
I tell myself that he passed to ease my own conscience. He was killed.
Killed at 23, for Dayton spokes on a 1990 Thunderbird he dreamed of
cruising down the Western Ave. back home from his college stint in
Sacramento.
Killed out of envy, greed, starvation, desperation, acclamation,
but killed just the same. The reason never mattered;
only what remained.
I thought my story was redundant,
that my pain was invalid.
that his death was merely statistical,
a ho-hum story of another black soul claimed by the ills of the streets
like a voucher, as if it was never his life, as if he never had that right
inherited like overbites and lazy eyes. as if me asking my mother "how
did he die?", "what is death?" wasn't reason enough to have my shirt
drench with tears back in 3rd grade when Mrs. Saxon asked what I was
doing to celebrate Father's Day. As if that's what a kid should expect to
experience. As if I didn't spend much of my life wondering the man I
could've been or the man I wasn't without him here.. He left a beautiful
daughter and a capricious and enigmatic son that would endure, 18
years after his death before he'd see his sister again. and 22 years before
he'd exalt his cries of his fallen father. he is missed. and he is impossible
to forget.

burden.

I can feel the weight of my presence,
morbidly surrounding my favorite things and people.
As if, things would be better without that tingling feeling
of obligation to understand my pains or my disconcerting plights
eating their nerves like parasites, injecting their veins with empathy for
my frailty. I can see the air escaping their body with every sigh,
the drag of their knuckles across the pavement
as their posture droops with the stench of regret
exhuming from their pores.
They're not bad people.
But everyone has a limit.
Everyone breaks;
we may be resewn,
reupholstered,
and re-purposed,
but oh do we break.
And I know it is only a matter of time before they do what humans
often do.
And I don't want their stories birthed
from guilt and shock that I know,
nor do I want the confirmation that
my fears and pessimistic thoughts are real..
because I don't blame them.
I can't blame them for not sacrificing their joy,
and their peace, as I have.
I cannot force them to find new ways to smile at life,
Nor can I ask them to adjust for my sake.
I understand that though they will never say it verbally,
their eyes gloss at the distance; and the distance can be daunting.
I accept if the weight of my presence may be overbearing.

space

I'm very protective of my space.
I don't want a lot of people in,
changing my thermostat,
breaking things,
overstaying their welcome.
I've been prone to hoarding.
I would collect bonds compulsively.
Because of that—
I've had to learn to let go
by being raided, emotionally.
So at times I have to protect myself with distance —
for my energy understands how I can get when
I become an open house for outside sources.

the mask.

I'm a prodigy at hiding pain,
I've done it my whole life.
It's all about honing a neutral mood.
That way they won't notice I'm grinding my teeth
to endure the lacerations my life
masterfully fences across my soul.
But it doesn't mean I don't feel the blood
seeping through my shirt from the wounds.
Or that I don't use the shower to drown
out the whimpers that accompany my tears.
Or that I wasn't holding this blade ever so closely
to my neck as I called you and let it kiss my throat
before backing out like prepubescent angst —
wanting, but not ready.
It doesn't mean I haven't lied to people and told them
these scars were just stretch marks.
It's not that I don't feel pain.
I just know how to hide it.

stonewall confessions.

Veganism didn't cure their depression.

Yoga didn't stop their pain.

Do we even know the cure?

Do we ever stop and ask ourselves what we're chasing?

A long life is a myth until you've lived one.

What's good health when you hate yourself?

I forgot I'm not supposed to say that.

Positive vibes only.

I'm told I'm killing my body like it's their business,

I'm told I'll be sorry as if I didn't know pain

before Jack and Mary found me sulking in a beach parking lot

that one night work and "love" had me calling Earl at the thought of

having another thought ever again.

I know they're merely positive steps.

I wish you didn't tell me how bad my life is and

will be until I find your vegan God or Buddha, or Jesus.

I wish you really were trying to help and not punch your ticket to

wherever our souls journey to next.

you, you

You ever wonder how much of
your stress is perpetual?
Or how many times you've placed yourself on
pedestals on the backs
of your peers' mishaps, failures,
misdirection, misinformation, and demise.
if it's your fear,
apprehension or condescension that ghostwrite your choices?
Or if your conviction or stubbornness defines you?
I guess I say this to ask..
Are you the *you* — you think you are?

c.

I see war stories painted on windows of empty buildings.
Pain echoed through the vibrations of the 100,000 odd souls that were
born and bred in the concrete kingdom of Inglewood. Ostracized and
stigmatized, written off in the wombs of our mothers, a chance is all
we wanted, even if we didn't know why.
I see scorned faces with the lust for gardens abundant in iridescent
pastures that were boosted in songs with cardinal rules of only having
value in life if we had it, because the ones back home either burned
whenever the sun came or nestled between the graves of past souls that
tried their hand in this involuntary game
we've come to know.
I see myself trapped on an island with painted backgrounds that look
endless, enticing me to reach for a life I may never see, but the idea
keeps me paddling with Nike trainers,
because I spent my last couple leaves on it instead of a paddle.
I see death certificates written with the tongues of vapor-victims who
claimed their ships should be more equipped than X, Y, and their
cousin, Z. I see faces dressed in the same skin as mine in warfare they've
been made to play in from generations of bone-deep conditioning in
the concept that only one of us will make it off this island built from
concrete to the ones that are only miles, but feel oceans away from us.
I see warlords in chariots that mask themselves in the colors of our
rivaled warriors, in voyeur, mocking the battle tactics, sweeping
through the ranks, devouring the remains. I see pain; I see hatred, of
this world, of self. I see a child laughing for no reason other than the
fact that I'm looking at them.
I see hope, I see purpose, I see reason.
I see love; of this world—
of self.

young king

Young King
your crown has been attacked by so much.
But they've told you not to cry about it.
To be a man is to be strong.
And to be strong - they say -
is to hide your emotions.
So you take those proverbial bullets
with the pride you were told to
always carry and never swallow.
But they never taught you how to be human.
They never taught you
the strength in the tears you sealed away.
Or the beauty in expressing those emotions.
(And)The power in your honesty
that would fuel your passion.
They feared your potential and constructed ways to withhold the truth.
That you were bred from royalty.
The evidence is that rich, sun-cooked skin.
Don't let this world silence your emotions.
It wants you that way..to just be a vessel.
It's okay to speak on love,
it's okay to not be a dominant personality and it's okay.
You can be sensitive. You can smile. Not smile.
You can be unconventional, you can be soft, and still be great.
This world has depicted you as beasts.
But you are much more graceful and majestic than they believe.
Young King. Stay true.
I'm rooting for you.
Reclaim the kingdom
that resides in you.

prisoner of past

You've let the past cut you for too long.

You've skipped your favorite songs or—
skipped over pages in your journal
so you wouldn't be reminded.
You pause when their name
is uttered and swallow your tongue
so you won't shout out the
demons you so vehemently kept in
like an over-packed suitcase.
But why be such a prisoner to your past?
It's like you've arrested yourself
because when those feelings
are free you have nowhere to run.
You never need to run, release yourself and walk.
Walk with confidence that
though your past is a part of you,
you are not its prisoner.

like voicemails to myself.

You are beautiful.
You are one that feels intensely
And loves immensely.
There is no shame for bearing that heart of yours,
it will change lives.
You shouldn't listen to what this world says, you know. There's
someone out there begging to see that crooked smile behind your lips.
They'll know your scent, your secrets, your mannerisms. Someone will
love the way you turn everything into a beat on some solid inanimate
surfaces and beat box your nervousness away. They'll be enamored by
your quips on any given subject. They will love your willingness to share
your sensitivity and your little poems about them, written in jubilation
for their existence. That spirit will emit an aura they'll want to be
around, even when they can't help themselves. But know none of this
matters if you won't get your head out of your ass, look in the mirror
and love all of those things you think are so shitty about you. You are
special, one of a kind, because you are you.

enough

I don't love myself enough, at times.
I forget the lessons gifted vicariously
through myself unto loved ones.
I attack motives,
and bury victories with vehement cynicism.
It's never good enough, for me.
It never lasts long enough.
It never feels.. real enough.
I anticipate the fall before the jump.
I'm not "sure" enough.
There's always a catch right?
There's always something waiting to
trip you at your feet before you reach the finish line.
I should know better.. I do.
Sometimes, I forget.

flowers

I've been finding myself
closer to the flowers.
Humans can be fickle.
Their energy can be draining.
But all flowers do is give life.
And right now, my soul needs life.
We're moving too fast,
too concerned with keeping up with ideas, perceptions, etc.
We don't slow down enough.
Flowers aren't something you can admire quickly. You have to stop,
assess every intricacy of their petals-- the stories their growth tells, in
order to appreciate its presence. I wish we treated ourselves more like
the flowers I admire. Maybe we'd see more beauty, maybe we'd
understand each other just a bit better, if nothing else.

self-seeker

I've come to adorn the way I search within;
How I'm constantly looking
for ways to discover
the depths of me.
I'm addicted
to my own energy.
It is my innate source of light;
my connection with the Most.
I learned through my trials,
that I am my savior;
my pick-me-up.
And that is a beautiful responsibility.

felt

Some want to be seen.
Others want to be heard.
I want to be felt.
I want to seep through your skin.
Travel your veins and
stimulate your senses.

I want your heart to skip
a beat from my energy.
For your soul to quake
in my presence.
I want to be felt in ways
no physical realm can fathom.
That only our spirits can translate
the effect of me.

You may not see me clearly.
You may not understand me fully.
But none of the above
is required to feel me, undoubtedly.

the plight in chasing mirages (interlude)

I understand that plight is necessary.
Like fire to the rain forest,
sometimes the only way to change is in a burning blaze.
I understand that love itself may be potent in pure, that it is a drug that
most people can't just handle on its own.
I understand that in my struggles finding love,

that a search in itself is futile.

Love finds you. It seems quite fickle in the way it chooses its partners,

but its eagerness is what always keeps you rooting for it.

I mean even love has to love love right?

Why else would it pair up with strangers just to experience it?

Why does it feel like fate when our eyes lock with what seems like the

better half of ourselves making a grand entrance in our lives to change

everything? Why is it something we are still searching to define?I can't

say that I've always welcomed its tour dates. Sometimes I just didn't

have the room in my home, I didn't have enough food to feed it.

I grew tired of not knowing when it was coming and when it was

going. Because too often it left too damn soon.

Too often was I too bruised to even answer the door. Love never came

on its own, it invited fear, envy, greed, anger, pain, and arguments over

text messages with all caps to let the other know we're pissed. that's the

thing with love, it holds no bias, no prejudice to whom it visits, maybe

how, but never whom. But how else would we know love if it weren't

for the clear signs of the visitors that ain't..

even heartbreak has a place, a reason to follow up the whys.

MARIGOLD

I know that plight is necessary.
I know that love is inevitable,
I'm still learning how to deal with both when they cross paths.

II:
CHASING MIRAGES

potent

Be careful in falling for those
that wish to dilute you.
You are to be loved
at your most potent.

the lies our mind tells

And of course I'd be up this early
with my thoughts piercing unrequited truths..
Writing things you probably
no longer care to read..
Believing your heart would sail my way in search of light
and I'd be the house rooted from rocks that yearn for
the ocean's embrace shining with elation because you realized
I was always where you needed to be, your guide, your home,
your love.. that is — if you let me tell it.

wannabe hero

I tried to save a soul, once.
No one warns you
how scorched you'd be;
reaching to pull them
from that hellish pit.
The cuts from each lie
that whelp your skin.
How their tender kiss would be
a contractual agreement;
hiding the fine print
as you sign on the dotted line.
It isn't mentioned
how their demons
would become yours,
and haunt you in their place..
..It will be your on-call duty.
requested when needed.
A subsequent intern,
constantly chasing them;
cleaning the destruction
left in their trail as they
flee from accountability.
Sleepless nights,
catering to self-inflicted wounds.
You transform
to their emergency room nurse.
Healing past gashes never sutured.

Yes, I tried to save a soul, once.
I was never told
that the entire time,
you'll be trying to save them,
from themselves.

confessions

If I admitted I missed you,
Would you hold it against me
if I confessed my wants
for your aura adjacent to mine..

thursday.

I'm the over-lover type,
Who dresses themselves
head-to-toe in their heart.
I never had a problem bearing myself
in the radical name of love.
But perhaps I was too boastful of my ability to warm you,
that you never felt it necessary to
wear your heart for me to see.
Maybe it was that one night, that night you laid across
my lap as if you paid rent in kisses.
You must've caught yourself slipping again.
Seeping back into a love you left buried beneath
your rib-cage to die like charred lungs.
Or is it true what they say,
"when it's real, it never fades"
..we just..keep it dormant.
Or in some cases, hidden.
Could it be that our love still sits in our chests,
yearning to be released;
blissfully unaware of the havoc wreaked?
That's what I'm telling myself, at least.
An over-lover's mind never sleeps,
so every possibility comes to creep.

undead.

It was apparent in our dialect; we grew apart long before we acknowledged its death. awkward silences followed by jaded sighs. it was only a matter of time before it would be euthanized. we've been here before. parked, soaked in tension over the moonlight on crenshaw in my mother's car. i called myself drowning out the sounds of my heart sinking and the gulps of my throat with small talk..yet..you hardly spoke. and when you did, bullets escaped your mouth; crucifying my emotions. executing my hope. burying me in my least favorite suit of despair. you told me of your spring plans.ibaited the inevitable chess match; asking where you'd be. we both knew. we both knew where you'd be. we both knew what that meant. we both knew i didn't have a say, but we both know I'm stubborn. so i was the one grabbing for the defibrillator, damning it to hell for dear life, pumping its chest, breathing into our fallen love as if it mattered. but the plug was pulled before i could park, the time of death punched in and the coroner only minutes away. we both knew that I'd never let go, but we both knew it was long gone before i could hold on.

addiction

You aren't aware of how addicted you are,
Until the drug leaves, and your body holds memories
deeply infused into your blood that you begin
to shake from reminders of how it once felt.

lust gods

With makeup smeared, from tears of absence.
Clinging to previous encounters;
she worshiped him.
He was a deity to her pleasures.
Her savior from deprivation.
and every night she called out to him.

Fleeting passion felt like dope to her womb
Raw love, potent.
Unsaturated contact that not everyone can handle.
She needed him; his touch --
to survive the night, in her eyes.

Her physical savior; her tangible prophet.
Her sober mind despised her sacrilegious inhibitions.
But the night would return.
and so will her call for physical salvation.

sip and slip

I'm here Hoping this liquor drowns the sounds of these memories,

It's because of you that I'm imprisoned by own mind,

I ask God why it has such a fixation on you.

Sip again, Slip again.

Mirages that fade through my fingertips.

With Schizophrenic murmurs of your voice.

I still remember you telling me I needed to get it together.

Sip again, Slip again.

I'm here Daydreaming that your touch becomes my melatonin.

With your smile settling as my serotonin.

But you always hated my insomnia.

I miss your nectar curing the tormented thoughts of

self-worth that eat my core like vultures on a corpse.

I miss your touches that felt like crutches affixed

to my body to keep me upright every time I welcomed the fall

because the fall called my hotline begging me to meet her,

and I was so used to her calling my name.

But you were always there to remind me

that I was so much more than failure,

so much more than my pain,

and a sip of you one last time could

do me better than calcium ever has.

And sober meant feeling it.

Sober meant the mountains

I painted would melt away.

And you would be what you've been for so long, now:

just a memory.

Just a moment I'll never reclaim.

Just a high I'll never achieve.

MARIGOLD

Sober meant

I failed again to reach the peak.

No those mountains must've

been too steep.

I'll lie to myself with the idea

that all I required was the right equipment,

if I just get back on my feet...

but being sober was like loose gravel..

Sliding me down to reality,

no kicking me down to reality.

I don't want to be sober,

let me fly, even if the mountains

and skies are fake.

Let me dream of that world

I used to taste.

But..

I'm lying...

You know I'll obsess again..

Looking to you to clean this mess, again.

Telling you over and over that I can just be friends.

And we both know you'll just plan your escape, again.

If only we could just pretend.

I'll just sip again.

Slip again.

crutch

Your were my crutch,
Preventing my weak
self from falling.
And you knew it.
You hated it.
You yelled
"What about me?..
how can I expect you
to be my strength when
I'm the one holding you together?"

I called myself being good at this.
It was just so natural to call on you.
I felt as though you could take on my demons
and not resent my cries for you to slay them.
I told myself I could defeat yours with ease,
but I wasn't prepared.
Yours were far more advanced.

But love wasn't enough to stop them,
Love alone could do so much.
You were my crutch,
But I was your prison.

aftertaste

I let my tongue massage
the roof of my mouth.
Because you're still here.
At least, that's what it tastes like.
You've been gone for umpteen days,
yet you're still here—
teasing my senses.
Having me relive my addiction of you.

say.

i want a say,
i want a chance to feel it first
before you come to jolt my
curiosity with your tempered skin
gently laid against mine.
i want to take charge of when
i get to want it, not be a drone to
my inhibition and your aroma.
i want my wants to
no longer want you.

home (too)

I don't want to be the bridge,
I'm tired of being a tour guide for what love could feel like,
tired of taxi'n lovers to the arms
of others that may be more capable.
I want to be the destination, your holy grail, your mission
accomplished, your everything, too.
I don't want to be alone on an island of my insecurities,
feeding from doubts falling from the tree,
too afraid to climb, discern, and pluck the good ones out;
settling for the weaker bits that are too acidic for my body to process
because I'm conditioned to eat this poorly
without care for the consequences..
for once—
I want to be the love
someone can't wait to come to.

lonely.

The amount of attention never
cured the loneliness,did it?
They wanted you for their own reasons.
Your body, your down-to-earth personality,
or some fantasy they've fabricated in
their minds that you "complete" them.
They showered you with affection,
gifts, declarations of their affinity for you in poems,
latched to your interests, so that maybe..
you'd look at them with stars bleeding
from your eyes and be convinced their love was
what you required all along like a missing link,
or finding the exact change in your sock drawer
for the delivery man at your door.
They never asked what you wanted,
What about you?
What if you didn't want a love
that obsessed over your very existence?
What if you wanted a love that was built mutually,
and not from the idea of another?
What if you didn't wish for anyone to fall in love with you at all?
And no matter how much they say they love you,
Who was willing to delve into the you that wasn't a fantasy?
Who really wanted to see the leaves fall
from the abundant tree that is
the you they so desperately pluck from?

Who would still care for you if you
didn't love them the same way you loved them?
And because of that, you haven't felt truly connected
with another soul to that magnitude in quite some time..
The attention you received was nice,
but it never cured the loneliness..
Did it?

under/over-lover

Your secret under/over lover.

your pique of interest when

all options are vexed.

your understudy, when the rest didn't study hard enough,

your sure thing, in case of emergency break glass, wash day lover.

Could I ever be the epicenter of your joy,

the anxiousness that filled your mouth

and rose your cheeks when you thought of me.

More than your temporary fix,

your "in the meantime",

sacrificial void filler.

More than the one you'd let go when they decided to see

everything I already saw in you,

and they learned the right things to say again,

and your swooning brought you back to your knees.

Will I ever be more than your secret under/over lover,

awaiting the call when your pillars fall,

and you find your love craving mine.

disconnect

Disconnect. Lost time.
Emotions that have
since calloused through enduring
trials & misadventures of
love stripped of its innocence;
like a child witnessing their parent's last breath.
Disconnect. Dilated pupils. Zoned mind.
Reflections of experiences that
I've chalked up to lessons in hindsight.
Empty promises, temporary forevers.
Though, in the moment they were
deeply embedded inside of me.
molding & submerging my subconscious into bliss.
Disconnect. Numb.
I forgot what it is to feel.
To have another's skin
pressed against mine in the name of love.
Our energies intertwined in passionate gropes.
I miss the boundless conversations,
Where we'd delve into each other's intellect.
With Laughter coated with reminders of
why we fell in love.
I miss the Companionship: our moral support
packaged with tough love and warm encouragements.
Disconnect. Distorted memories. Painful mementos.
Perhaps I do feel,
after all.

honesty

"Honesty.."
You expressed through a sigh,
"Why does honesty seem elusive?"
You wanted a lover that kept their word
even if it just meant being on time.
You said you were too young to be so accustomed
to the lies men told to keep you.
I suppose you were asking rhetorically, of course,
But when I see you, I could see how men would long to tell tales
that could morph your eyes into non anatomical hearts.
You never quite felt real,
a character a part of some foreign mythology
that somehow found its way into real life
in the form of a round-the-way goddess,
they probably likened you to Cleopatra, Neffertiti,
you know- something to deify you; make you blush, reaffirm those
thoughts that often come fresh from the shower,
or fresh from you r resurrection of self-loathing.
perhaps that's why they professed lives they never lived
or lifestyles they could never maintain.
They wanted to match the folklore you personified;
because you weren't ordinary,
and ordinary lovers could never match your presence.
But you simply wanted honesty,
not the excuse of your place on their perpetuated pedestals.
But a love that was transparent, absent of the cryptic signals
you've become too used to crying over. I couldn't blame you.

handle

They don't get it, you said.
Nor do they ever try to.
You feel that everyone wants
that light of yours yet they never
reach the end of the tunnel.
"How can they crave fire,
yet fear the touch?".
I wish i had an answer for you.
But simply, most will never be
equipped to clasp your infernos.
Some are better suited to watch from afar.

Its human nature to yearn for what we may not be ready to handle.

martyrs.

You've grown tired of the martyr lover.
The "make it about you while saying
I'm making it about me" lover,
because it was always something you owed them.
You were never good enough,
yet they threw themselves on the line to love you
 "the right way".
You grown tired of the superficial, sacrificial, fake deep,
underwhelming lover that thought
you'd simply pause your life so they can grow.
You've grown tired of being the muse and the goal,
as if you were prize for people to display like
medals and check off a bucket list.
You've grown tired of debts assumed by another's insecurities.
All so the lover feels entitled to have because
they're a "good person".
You've grown used to loving yourself just fine,
you no longer care for objections.

lust, love, and in-between.

You favored love that gave your legs
their own soul and buckled your knees.
For your atoms to dance beneath your skin,
and your hips to reach for the ceiling
while you bit your lip in search of breath.

You wanted love with a lover
that was as gentle
and patient with your body
as they were with your heart.
But knew when turbulence was needed.
You wanted a love that could make you spill avalanches,
but would stay to keep you warm
when the blizzard arrived.
Such a hard medium to find.

the user

You use 'em all,
'til you've had your fun.
Then you rotate,
'til they've lost their run.
How many lovers have
come undone,
just to see your morning sun.

seasons

I adored you like the flowers admired the sun;
needing your light and warmth to reach my potential.
But it was the same light that blinded me to you;
and in the end I was burned --
scorned by the mark you left on my soul.

I forgive you.
After all, even the seasons
forgive each other.
Spring forgives Winter for its frigidness
by shedding light among the world,
blooming plains of sunflowers and trees of orchards.

The Summer forgives Spring for the pollen
it spreads and the runny noses it leaves
with its warm embrace and gives
the ocean waves to dance in joy.
The Fall forgives the Summer for its eventual sweltering
presence and wildfires by parading us with calming rain.
And the Winter forgives the Fall for drenching the streets
and dragging kids back to school by coating the earth
with quilted snow, sweaters and
peppermint tea while bundled near the fireplace.
So I'll forgive you by loving the one after you
Immensely and unconditionally.
For they too will be in need of Spring
after the unforgiving Winter.

"i hope you're well"

"I hope you're well."
That line will never change.
We understand that we both still care.
That we both still love each other.
But the bridge may never be salvaged.
Yes, every blue moon, I'll miss you.
Not intentionally, and not because a new love is insufficient.
It's just the nature of the beast, right?
When we love deeply, it's bound to embed in our veins.
And you'll probably always remain a part of me.
But it's probably better this way,
That we love in passing,
with simple messages just seeing if we're alive,
because we remember there was once a time
we were a reason we lived for each other.
So I hope you're happy,
I hope peace has kissed your heart
and I hope you're well..

chasing love songs (interlude)

Chasing gets old.
After awhile, you feel gravity increase and your knees scream for peace
as you push and push, dragging the balls of your feet with futile hope
and retreating passion.
loving was never supposed to be easy.
You know this.
every time, you knew this.
But you keep on.
you keep on for what it does to shitty days and sleepless nights, for the
way it turns doubt to stone, and your worries to forgotten daydreams.
you keep on because love says it's worth it, and as much as you claim for
certainty, the hope—the possibility that it intercepts your skin and
palliates your heart supersedes the times it seems to devour your soul,
grope your esteem, claim it needs and won't even call you back..
but I've been through this for a long time..
I can feel the grays of this journey accumulating, I want to get there.
I just feel so tired, and it feels a bit harder, less possible, less fulfilling,
but I know I'm in my head.
I know love is the answer, and all it brings.
I'm still learning its tune.
So love teach me your hymns, teach me your somber melodies, your
sensual ballads, your angelic nastiness, your subtle bass, your infectious
groove lines, that make me pine for your release like an adorned
musician who's taking too damn long to release their next masterpiece.
Teach me your songs so that I serenade you to stay.

III:
LOVE SONGS

fragile (she)

She isn't afraid to be passionate.
I love that about her.
How she wears her wings
without fear if they'd be clipped.
She's also fragile.
And it should be understood.
That it's her delicacy
that steers her strength.
You'd be unwise to count her out.
She isn't perfect; but she lives.
She dares to go beyond what's
within reach to find herself.

She's in search of something —
ultimately purpose;
but by her own definition.
She cared not for how she was perceived.
She moved with unapologetic conviction.
A slayer of presumption, ruler of self.
You see she is, poetry, smooth jazz, weary and beautiful blues;
a phonetic soliloquy in her unique rhythm.
The kind that reminds you when the language was delicate--
but just hard enough to vibrate that cavernous pit in your chest.
She is an experience.
She is poetry.
She varies in size.
Not physically,
but existentially; in context.
& like poetry, I absorb her in all forms.

abalone cove

I trek to your abalone cove.
You've kept yourself hidden from most.
Strong enough to take the tide,
but open enough let someone willing to search, in.
Dark enough to keep your secrets,
but lit enough for your details.
They all want you, but you're a trip.
And not enough like to venture for lasting experiences..

roots (legs)

God-carved curves,
dipped in caramel,
your roots hold stories,
they speak of how they've kept you up on days
you wanted to buckle and give in.
how they help your hips sing along
to your favorite melodies,
and bridge your mountains to the plains of your fruit.
your roots symbolize your ability to bend,
fold in ways that you must, but rarely break.
remember that you are beautiful and resilient,
and that those roots will always remind you.

girls from LA

I fell for you.
I could name it all,
That vernacular you possessed,
Or maybe just the way you reminded
me of a me I never felt safe traveling alone to.
So you scared me at first.
In that,
"I just know she'll devour every fear I hold sacred"
kind of scared.
I didn't like how you could deconstruct every word that
clumped my throat without making an effort.
But you had me.
And you just knew,
I would follow you everywhere.
Even if I fell too deep
and you climbed out,
I'd find the scent you left stamped on me.

that bar.

I remember taking you to that bar.
It was your first time,
and you weren't much of a drinker so I ordered for us,
we joked on how the bartender was a better looking
Ben Affleck.
Breaking ice was always my strong suit,
even though I was known as the quiet one.
We tried something sweet and talked on
how we'd make every movie better with our tweaks
knowing damn well we didn't know a thing on making one.
I saw love in simple things, in your nervousness,
in the way your leg waddled because you were anxious.
We both felt it but we just played it off.
Okay, maybe it wasn't love yet.
But our bodies knew something we didn't,
and I love it when it gets like that,
when we move like waves, no effort...just..being.
Afterwards, we just sat in the car,
with silence between us as my phone
played the soundtrack for the night.
Your head found a home on my shoulder,
You blew dust off of thoughts you had
shelved just for moments like this;
moments where you could just be...you.
But you soon drifted to sleep, as you always do.
And I continued to play the ambiance, as I always do.
I swear I'd freeze time just to have that a bit longer.

shouted

Your eyes shouted
what your mouth couldn't.
You wanted clarity, a signal
of whether to slow down
or to floor it.

Instead there was simply silence;
piercing through your conscience,
with tension and anticipation
rising under each word unsaid.

Perhaps the answer didn't
need to be so transparent.
You were here;
and in this moment
the ride felt too intoxicating,
too blissful, for it stop now.

numbsoul

You had this amazing way of
shutting out the world when you felt down.
But as much as I admired that, I knew the danger.
I knew how shutting the world off had
damaging effects, long-term. How being numb meant
you didn't feel the love that whispered at the
nape of your neck, the joy that rained on your skin,
the peace that filled your lungs.
You're not wrong for shutting out the world
when you're down, but you miss out on
so much more when you allow them to win.

love for the hopeless

You told me you didn't believe
in happy homes.
I mean — your parents split
when you were 2,
so who could blame you.
Now you shun commitment,
so circumvention
is your favorite audible.

You told me commitment was
against our nature.
That we're prone to
trashing lovers after the scent
of limerence wears off.

You held these ideals since you've
never experienced it yourself.
Or at least..you were afraid to.

What if you've been running away
this whole time from what was meant
to heal those hashes you've
accumulated dodging love.

But love is everywhere around you.
It's what you breathe.
What you consume.
Whether you believe it or not.
Love exists and it's fighting
for you even when you doubt it.

like I do

I wish you loved you like I do..
You peel back your skin to suffocate
your veins with words untrue.
An unbeliever of the murals
I paint of you.
You must understand my adoration.
For your essence is
to be ingested in all forms
the human can feel.
You are more than poetry,
more than sonnets, songs,
illustrations or language can describe.
But you are life: Imperfect, but invaluable.
A billow of emotion and beauty
bottled and served in the physical.
I daydream of days where you aren't
colorblind to the gold that emits from your skin.
Or how the sun and moon both permeate within you.

It isn't cliche to say you're beautiful, sometimes;
it's simply the truth.
You are love.
I wish you loved you like I do.

must be you

It must be your mind:

>   That I've booked getaways to
>   and built summer homes
>   and winter lodges in
>   to find the pieces of myself
>   I could never quite make sense of
>   before you came.

It must be your heart:

>   That seems to sear
>   my defensive frigid walls
>   with just a touch,
>   no matter how well I've built them.

It must be you:

>   To have found loving such a
>   tormented and jaundiced compilation
>   of flesh worth it to let me stay.
>   I may never know,
>   but I'll forever be indebted
>   to the love that is you.

because of you

I didn't come here because
it would be easy.
I didn't tell you I loved you because you would
magically rid me of my worries,
or that I fantasized about some happily ever after
where you and I lived that perfect life that only those born in
impoverished conditions could surmise
from the depths of their plight.
I crave you.
The words you only say to yourself those nights
you're convinced the universe hasn't a clue. (Or)
Those laughs that go unnoticed among
your own inside jokes.
I crave you.
I crave your good mornings,
and the mornings you lack
the energy to commit to anything other than
making love to your bed
and climaxing to the thought of a lazy Sunday being all yours.
Or the intricacies your daily mechanics possess,
Even the way you cradle your left cheekbone when you're nervous,
I crave your hellos like addicts crave highs.
Even the mundane things you do are done magically.
I look at you and sit in awe at how someone could
feel so healing with just a glance.
You're so special without doing anything extraordinary.
And it's not that you haven't been so,
but you've just mastered the art of being love.
I came here to love because of you.

my stupid little poem

Would you mind my mind,
My crazy little mind,
When it needs time to unwind,
In search of time it could never find,
And space it'll never replace
When it thinks it needs to escape.

Would you mind my faults,
my stupid little faults,
as my ego runs rampant
yet is easily damaged.
'Cos I fear my own conceit,
Therefore retreat with responses
that appear meek.

Would you mind my hypocrisy,
When I proclaim I hate
what I've never tasted, with wasted
moments on thoughts that are aimless.
Shameless rhetoric professed
in faulted discernment.

If you don't mind me,
Tender yet jagged me,
I'll give you all of me.
Internally, externally.
Eternally.

need (notes in inglewood)

You have life,
passion -- unafraid to tell me when I'm wrong,
checking the itinerary of my ego trips.
Pushing me when the cement
fills my shoes with stagnation.
Lifting me from the swamps
my doubts dwell in.
You don't allow me to quit on myself,
because you see beyond
the ceiling my conscience
places upon itself.
Never be afraid to
speak how you feel.
I need this.

3AM

I can be selfish.
I'll call you at 3am,
Wanting to get away and take you with me.
To experience every encrypted piece of my mind.
You'll have to forgive that, but you bring me relief, peace; hope.
That maybe, this hell on earth is subjective,
and when we share our journeys, we create heaven.

seep

Your kisses seep into my bones.
Your touch exalts my deepest angst.
I've traced you a million times
in my head.
And connected every freckle
on your warm skin.
You are chamomile tea
in human form; refreshing, healing,
yet it takes a tender pallet
to taste you at your most searing.

come

As the moonlight kisses your curves through the cracks of the blinds,
your moans play the soundtrack to our night.
Our bodies became vessels for what our souls were craving for.
I recall hints of lavender filled the room as I pollinated your womb.
Your whispers beckon you want it deeper.
I revel for the taste of you and your nectar;
Your quivering river.
Your hisses give signals that you wish to..
Over and over as I knock your doorbell..
Each squirm is an invitation to your blissful temple.
Where nirvana dwells and heaven
seems closer than it's ever been.
Many men sinned for just a hint of the body equivalent of gin and
heroine. Though few attain the patience to unearthed your Horus. I
promise to be contrary.
If I use my key to unlock your oceans,
you'll forever wish to arrive at this moment.
Over and over as I knock your doorbell..
Do you want it hard, as hard as I fell?
Or do you want it soft as pillows and pastels.
The legend tells that your oil well
grants wishes if you dive in it,
and my intentions is to make your
heavenly peach my daily nutrition.

apex.

the apex of my tongue knows the taste of your curves.

I remember the taste of your curves with the apex of my tongue.
You are a flavor one craves in primal conviction; innately.
In ways that I wish to engrave across your lines with every soliloquy that
pervades my mind. this tongue knows the way you fix your hips to
match its cadence. knows how to unlock your tides with subtle strums
while your moans become the melody of our ballad.
i write you songs of honey, caramelized atop your flesh like confections
in sweltering summers; confessing wants of your ambrosia to emanate
from you like seiches when the moon isn't so shy.
you tell me without words how you quiver to my interludes, melt
between my bridges and fall to your knees at each libretto that flows
from my lips in harmony with you.
i know the extended plays your body yearns to move to.

vibrations

Those vibrations you exude; both passionate and intense;
being engulfed in you is such a sensation
and that energy of yours is what I lust for.
I'm blessed to delve into realms with a soul daring to take the trip
where ecstasy comes to breed peace and egos suffocate.
I feel a rush through my fingertips with mere thoughts of you
from that night you came in Niagara's, Euphrates, Nile's;
tracing them like braille, decoding your wants
to bring you back to moments where these feelings are so engorged in
our energies shared. I let these vibrations speak what my mind and
body are translating.
The orgasmic, tantra love-driven lust I can feel tingling your body.
Your posture gave me chills; the way it pronounced your confidence.
Speaking in a language of its own that you accorded no translation for,
it just had to be understood.
I admire a lover that knows they've got it without having to tell me. I
could feel it coursing through me every time you spoke.

You must be the moon.

Only the moon could make my adrenaline rush like waves inside me.

With your body pressed against mine like bare feet gently touching

marble floors as if we're testing if the water is too cool too hot or just

right, I drift into dimensions I thought only existed as exaggerations in

passing. I've heard from those that have felt the luscious lips

of their lover often speak of this taste.

This opulence your body is soaked in gives me what mine

lacks like a virgin that's never been kissed

or deaf ears that have never known sound

or blind eyes that have never seen the face

of the one that made their heart crack open their chest

and soar to where only stars and other makings

of the galaxy admire flawed humans in flawed love that has a certain

beauty in the right angles.

Make me rise to you, until the tides fall,

and the stars kiss the oceans we've made anew.

Perhaps it's why I find myself in dire need of more..of you.

mirror

I want you in front of the mirror.
I love it when it's intense,
where we can barely lock eyes, but we try.
And when we do, we erupt.
I love it when you make that face;
you know, that "what dimension are you taking me?",
"don't you dare stop" face.
I love it when I kneel behind to taste you
and you're scrounging for something to hold onto.
With your toes faintly touching the ground
and legs having convulsions as if
your soul is ascending to reach me.
This is more than love making.
This is much more.
the love is already here.

fi8ure

I tried to figure you out.
First mistake.
You need a love that will
appreciate your mystery,
caress your wonders and
revel in your isms.

like a fool

You were the one I was afraid to love.
We were friends before and I knew so
much of your past, I was afraid.
So I resisted.
I didn't want your smile to be
the greatest gift to kiss my subconscious.
I begged for your warmness not
to heal my frost-bitten cynicism,
that your love wasn't capable of making me feel content
yet so ambitious to explore you & I much deeper.
I was afraid. Like a fool I was afraid.
I would've missed out on the best love that
could've happened to me.
I wasn't supposed to love you,
How many times did I sell that lie to myself.
How long did I fight in a war that was aimless.
You were everything to me before
you became my everything.
You were a love I needed before
I could spell your name, correctly.
I've never met a smile that could
scare away my demons, 'til yours found me.
Or a spirit that calmed my frantic, psychoanalytic ways.
You brought joy in a bite size package
without even trying to conceal it.
And to think, I told myself I wasn't supposed to love you.

consistency

I don't need you to promise consistency.
We are flawed, love.
You won't always be there.
Nor could you always make me happy.
You are composed of flesh and bones.
Not wires and cords.
You will lie.
You will hurt me.
And I am fated to do the same.

So don't promise me your consistency.
Promise me your humanity.
That you will be the you I fell in love with;
with even more to love as our souls will grow.

happiness when..

i am happiness when
you kiss me to remain awake with you.
when you pout your lip at my leaving.
the kisses on my stomach you've never left as a joint decision.
when you exclaim your passions in a less preferred tone.
when you blame me for your forgetfulness.
i am happiness when you look in the mirror
and misplace your reasons to smile.
when "you are my world" aren't
enough words to remove your
veil from the truth.
when your shoulders are crying
out to give way to the weight of your worries.
i am happiness when you fear your days
and dread your sleep.
my love for you remains.
even when you don't feel deserving,
happiness remains, in spite of the rain.

death, taxes, (and loving you)

I love you
and I've never felt so mortal.
I never thought I could fear death.
blame youthful privilege for my arrogance.
but it wasn't till you told me 'good morning',
that I ever had a good one.
it wasn't till you fixed your hips to align with mine
like we were conjoined that I ever felt so connected.
I know this was supposed to sound like roses
cascading across your soul,
to speak of how invincible you make me, and you do.
I feel both heaven and hell from you,
both life and death, everything and nothingness.
I feel so much of you that at times I fear your smile,
your happiness, your scent, your scowl,
your pet peeves, your quirky habits, your everything.
so much that I'm afraid I'll sabotage it,
because I don't know how to have nice things.
so much, that I fear you'll smarten up like they all did
and leave while you have the chance.
I don't like this feeling, sometimes.
I don't like the idea of not having control of
where my mind and heart chose to rest.
the world is both fascinating and mundane;
I was once fine leaving this world with that fact.
But you've given me more reason to not want to let this world,
or any remnant of it go without you journeying whatever this all
means, with me.

dear black woman

Thank you for being you.
For not apologizing
for your magik.
For your divinity in
every shade of your melanin,
size of your body,
and mixture of your roots.
You are the essence.
Spirit.
Senses.
Spine.
The imagery of black ethereal.
Flavor of our culture.
You are life.
You are you.
And I thank you.

the woman

To some you are the ambitious woman.
Others you're a survivor
of a patriarchal apocalypse.
You are a warrior.
A lover.
A multi-colored collar worker.
To those oh-so special ones,
you are mom.
No one carries your burdens
with such beauty and resilience.
No one finds time to love
so many so openly.
No one takes on the world,
all while being a planet to others.
No one else saves the day
with a forehead kiss
and an open heart.
Like you.
You are everything.
Thank you.

chamomile love (interlude)

I think we find so much of ourselves in a new territory,
and what I mean by that is
when we are hitting these walls,

that's exactly what they are: **walls.**

A wall is of course a barrier,

which means naturally something must be beyond the wall,

it could be nothing, it could be everything, but sometimes we don't

know our limits until we hit those walls, and when that feeling you're

feeling, that I'm feeling, hits us..to me, it means we are at capacity.

We are at the limit of our current comprehension of self.

We must break that wall, and open up new terrain to traverse,

new plains to cultivate,

new ways to understand ourselves.

I say that all to say:

you are more than built for what's haunting you,

but you can also redefine your approach in finding

new ground for yourself,

a new way to cultivate your understanding,

and thus changing, evolving.

IV:
CHAMOMILE

to be said

There is something to be said about
climbing from the depths

of your misery to recover the love of yourself.

Getting to that particular point on your own feet

is much more meaningful than someone imposing

their will on you to get there.

anemone

Keep me safe.
I often drift when things go to waste.
I'm learning to clean my mistakes before I leave it to burn for another
safe house that's just another home "in the meantime".
Teach me growth in transition, teach me that the aches are worth it,
teach me that growth means stretching beneath the soil, severing
cracks with will. You tell me that the water (experience) is meant to
cleanse me and that I must learn to endure its pressure along with the
sun's searing light that will grace me with clarity.
I am your reason just as much as you are mine.
You cannot pull without my falling,
I cannot move forward without your pushing.
Protect me in my transition of resurrection and salvation.

you: the love story

You know what's incredible? I get to love me.
I think we should all appreciate the fact
that we get to love ourselves.
No one knows you like you.
No one knows those little nuances
about yourself better than you.
That day you decide to part your hair to the right
instead of the left because you felt like
that was a start of the "new you".
Or that show that for some reason you only watch and
that's a travesty to you because
"everyone should be watching this".
They don't get to see those random moments that you're shy
with yourself in the mirror and can't help but smile
even though you never really know why you're smiling.
You get to love you.
You are the love story you've been waiting on.

your worst enemy (you)

That stubborn pit in your chest
that holds promises left unkept
will never fill, love.
Isn't it obvious..
That hell was designed by you.
Cultivated by you.
You clung to lovers and dreams
you knew the ending to.
You knew your character died
in some way every time,
yet you sold yourself a pyramid scheme:
if you could convince someone
to love you the way you wished,
maybe they'd stay,
and you two will make children
built from that same love,
and they will find other lovers to love;
and just maybe, this idea could become
the family you always envisioned.
You never told yourself,
that love couldn't be forged that way..
so every person that crossed your path
wasn't really this symbol of faith,
rather this cruel marketing plan you
surmised without ever understanding
the hell you were digging,
the hell where only you
and those empty promises,
those sad love stories, would remain..

just like you

I know you very well.
I was just like you.
In ways, I still am.
I sat up in my bed,
head propped in between
both hands; staring through the wall,
searching for change too.
Breaking down every wall
I've built to ward off intruders
to only find myself alone in my castle.
I've feared uncertainty
like the antelope hearing
the lurking steps of a stalking prey.
I see through those dilated eyes
that you lost you; just like I did.
Your world has endured hurricanes
that took a part of you away
with each crashing wave.
You tried running until those legs gave;
until every breath felt like it brought you closer to death.
I know what that defeat smells like
charred on your skin.
That apprehension in your
quivering knees on starting over again;
those words hidden underneath your
tongue sharper than razor blades.

It's okay to be afraid.

I was just like you.

In ways, I still am.

If I'm proof of anything,

even in trying days;

If you learn to believe in you,

there's a way.

say your peace

You can't keep words or emotions bottled in.
You owe it to yourself to let it out.

Say your peace.
Never constrict your tongue to satisfy another's ego.
It only leads to your destruction.
From implosion to explosion.
Harboring resentment damages you
more than anyone else.
It's best to express that anger
or pain than to let it fester.
But with a purpose.
Express with a means to be understood.
With an intent to establish the field of
how others must respect how you feel,
what you do, and what you will and won't tolerate.

Set yourself free.

"who am I doing it for?"

I feel it's important that we reaffirm
that with ourselves,
every now and again.

It can be so easy at times
to lose our way or reason for our drive.
You may have pursued it
for yourself but then your partner
needed it, your friends needed it,
your mom, dad, family needed it.
Outside people, even.
And you start losing
all of the reasons
why you needed it.
I always say go for you first,
everything else is secondary;
because if you're not doing it
for yourself first,
then your heart is half in it.
And I've never seen anything
grow from a seed halfway in the soil.

hype

The hype won't save you.
It may feel good chasing the money;
lusting for it, marrying the idea of success.
But your soul knows the price.
You keep chasing the hype and all of sudden,
you look in the mirror
and can barely look at your own eyes,
your soul mourns for you.
And there will come a time
when even **you** can't recognize yourself.
I never wanted that,
I've seen what it does to people.
I've seen the soulless gaze,
I've seen the pain through their body language.
In the end, you only starve yourself
while the world feeds off of you.
Don't find yourself chasing anything that doesn't speak to you,
or feel that you have to emulate a wave just to maintain.
Treat yourself better, I promise you it ain't worth it.

artists

Artists, we are just like caged animals.
Our art is the cry for freedom
against a world we feel entrapped by.

And my art is avaricious .
You see, it must represent me,
speak the way I speak,
creak the way my soul creaks,
before anything.
If it can save the world's of many,
I am grateful.
But my art must save me first,
for it to be the hero to others.

people need people

People
  need
    people.
We move as if we're in this alone,
And forget to appreciate the
connections constructed with others.
We cannot tread our paths
without needing another for
the road itself to be paved.
Our very birth is due to the cooperation
of two souls sharing their bodies.
Energies are dependent.
In reality,
we cannot survive
from just our own.

Why else would our souls long
to be entwined with another?

Or what else would cause such a rush
through our bloodstream when we feel loved?

We need something.
We need someone.
We need each other.

cherish your growth.

There will come a day when you'll feel lighter,
and the energy that once held your spirit in contempt, fades.
I can't tell you when, but when it comes—
let it revive you,
for some of you has to go,
for you to be whole.

ABOUT THE AUTHOR

Daeizm is a writer from Inglewood by way of Jefferson Park, CA, a district located in South Los Angeles, CA.

Booking & Inquiries: daeizm@gmail.com

65975450R00061

Made in the USA
Charleston, SC
08 January 2017